Seasons of Earth and Sky

poems by

Karen Jones

Finishing Line Press
Georgetown, Kentucky

Seasons of Earth and Sky

Copyright © 2020 by Karen Jones
ISBN 978-1-64662-363-1 First Edition
All rights reserved under International and Pan-American Copyright Conventions. No part of this book may be reproduced in any manner whatsoever without written permission from the publisher, except in the case of brief quotations embodied in critical articles and reviews.

ACKNOWLEDGMENTS

My sincere thanks to the editors of these journals for their previous publication of the following poems:

Plum Tree Tavern: "Missouri River Cottonwoods", "Cormorants at Yaquina Bay"
River Poets Journal: "White Pine"
Tower Poetry Journal: "Lunar Eclipse", "Narrow Trail in April"

Publisher: Leah Huete de Maines
Editor: Christen Kincaid
Cover Art: Karen Jones
Author Photo: Karen Jones
Cover Design: Elizabeth Maines McCleavy

Order online: www.finishinglinepress.com
also available on amazon.com

Author inquiries and mail orders:
Finishing Line Press
P. O. Box 1626
Georgetown, Kentucky 40324
U. S. A.

Table of Contents

Narrow Trail in April 1

Owyhee Spiderlings 2

Bear Grass 3

Arctic Terns 4

John Day River Canyon 5

White Pine 6

Missouri River Cottonwoods 7

Teen Eagle 8

Lunar Eclipse 9

September Meadow 10

Big Leaf Maple Leaves 11

Ten Days on the Green River, Utah 12

Cormorants at Yaquina Bay 13

Madrone 14

Comet 15

Ice Bubbles 16

Sermermiut, Greenland 17

Bob Hunger's Place 18

December Snowshoe 19

Winter 20

Narrow Trail in April

Young cedar deepen
in creeksong, feather
wet, blue-green.

Deer stamps an arrowhead
soft in depression,
dog blackens her paws;
half-moons of horseshoes
print the earth raw.
Water in ditch
shivers milk-brown,
mirrors branches above
leaves drowned.

Salmonberry
perfumes magenta,
brown-shell fungus
frills the stump,
first dogwood flower
plays a dusk flute.

Owyhee Spiderlings

Wind-birthed from gossamer, parachuting to air
in silken launch of new life,

shining filaments polish the sky, waft in the breeze,
slant through rays of setting solstice sun.

When light is low, angled above rimrock,
their flight is revealed to our unpracticed eyes.

Drifting featherweights on diagonal draglines,
some catch a neighborhood sagebrush,

clump of bunchgrass, jumble of basalt.
Others fly high, on lifelines fine and strong,

long enough to cross a river canyon, a mountain,
weave a new orb on the other side.

Bear Grass

Between charred spires of fir,
Mountain Hemlock, Lodgepole Pine,

stalks rise from clumps of tough grass.
White breasts of blossoms open,

sway and tremble in the breeze,
float like clouds through burned forest.

Tiny beetles swarm the clusters.
Their antennae probe for depths of cream,

caress yet unopened petals.
Their nations feast in sweetness.

Arctic Terns

East wind blasts forty knots,
as they flutter and hover above the chop,
plummet and splash among whitecaps,

chatter and buzz in aerial ballet,
slim wings knifing through salt spray,
chasing intruders from their land

where fuzzy babes wait midst the uproar,
red mouths gaping, begging for more
fish gruel breakfast.

Now they rest together in a flock
on a beach of black basalt,
all facing one direction,

long forked tails, backs of pearl-gray,
hot red bills, black berets,
little sailors at attention.

Home is wind, a rocky shore,
sky above the cold, cold fjord,
endless grace of motion.

John Day River Canyon

Wind blasts up the gorge,
across meander and riffle of river,
slopes of rippling bunchgrass,
scars of rimrock and rockfall

where beat of heat, torrent of rain
erode turf and soil, sculpt stone
to spires, jumbled terraces,
cliff homes for falcon and eagle.

Wind, rain, wash of river
unearth the ancient lava flows,
mountain bones once hidden
beneath green-golden hills,

massive columns of basalt,
organ pipes of red and brown.
Stone feathers, broken faces,
their songs rise from underground.

White Pine

Branches wide to wind and sky,
your feathers brush the heavens
in softness and strength
high above the jumbled shore.

Tree of old, now you return,
scatter your seed in your native land
where the wild cry of the loon
echoes across waters.

Missouri River Cottonwoods

Thunder growls under Meadowlark song.
Clouds pile the horizon, the river glides.

Cottonwoods, ancient children, lean
along the bank. Their roots seek cool waters.

Rugged bark covers massive trunks.
Limbs, dry old bones, full of gnarls and knobs,

bend to the ground like knees of giants.
Dead twigs tangle in cracks of heartwood.

Young boughs, smooth and limber,
bounce and sway easy as a porch swing.

Leaves spin on long, flattened stems,
rain-patter in breeze. Finest of leather hearts,

they sparkle like sun on water, like haloes
of vibrant atoms, ever green in the drying wind.

Teen Eagle

He somersaults
into a cedar
beside his mother,
breaks branches, flaps
his rags of wings, teeters, finally
balances, then shakes,
pulls at his mottles of brown and white,
scratches an ear with a dinosaur foot,
snakes his neck, swivels his head,
eyelids flashing.

He will learn to land
without crashing, lift from treetops
without stumbling,
circle in thermals above the earth,
spar with the ravens. He'll grow his white head,
great yellow hook, talons strong enough
to break a man's bones.

But now, tousled near his mom,
he calls for food, pierces the sky
with his cries. She turns away, preens,
smooths a few feathers back into fans of flight.
A white puff of down from her breast
floats free, turns on the breeze.
It's time for him to fly to the waters,
cross the currents, fish the breathing tides, alone.

Lunar Eclipse

Traveling her ordered path,
moon passes through Earthshadow,
our million mile cone of dark
extending opposite the sun.

Our penumbra gnaws her silver,
our consuming core of black
devours her left eye, then her right,
and in a silent smothering

swallows up her Bay of Rainbows,
feasts upon her Lake of Dreams,
extinguishes the play of light
upon her face. And though it seems

we understand paths of darkness
out beyond, how shadows
circle, coincide, move on,
we don't recognize our own.

We shoot arrows, beat our drums,
scare away the wolf or jaguar.
We forget the moon's escape
is as certain as her capture.

September Meadow

Sun golds green, warms with bright blanket,
adorns my lashes with prisms.

Grasses, slender stems heavy with seed,
bow in the breeze, dance like prayer flags,
each a shining strand defined by light.

Dark clothed oaks stretch lichen fingers
across my path. Above, a vulture,
black, deep-keeled, rocks like a boat at sea.

Big Leaf Maple Leaves

Great leaves lose hold, blow free,
dance your first, last, eternal dance
down to the slow quicksand.

All summer you have greened
on the living bough. Now,
your riverbeds and watersheds
overflow with gold. Star the trail,
palm the soil with your generous hands.
Gold is your own color. You are old,
you are beautiful.

You are the golden skyfood
drifting to the earth, food
for those who await
the turning of the season,
food for the fruiting bodies
birthing under your replenished shawl.

Ten Days on the Green River, Utah

Raven call echoes off cliffs. Swifts circle
our canoe, cloud feathers dissolve to blue.
Time travelers following the waters,
we drift the river, its channels, meanders.

Clouds of sand gust across the beach.
The flat hums with ground-nesting bees.
A sheen of dust sticks to our sunscreened faces,
grit lodges in our ears and teeth.

I stand in silt shallows. Depths of mud suck
at my feet. Grain by grain, my footsteps erase
in the gentle, relentless wash. Bedloads drift
across the wide channel, build onto banks,

break away. Chunks of sand thunk into the river,
dilute to mud and slurry, deposit downstream.
In the evening, fine particles blow into our tent,
dust our sleeping bags. They'll cover us in time.

By day, we await rain under thunderous skies,
sheltered by an overhang of Navaho Sandstone.
The current pulls our canoe deeper through cliffs
of tilted strata, springs, lofty gardens.

Ancient Pueblo dwellings tuck under eaves
high above the water. Generations of stone rise
to meet us: Kayenta, Wingate, Cedar Mesa,
each layer the remains of an era. We gaze

upon ages of desert rock, river mud shale,
consider our future in stone, our clay someday
layered in a cliff, buried in thin strata, our world
a fossil of future's past, lithified, eroding.

Cormorants at Yaquina Bay

Along the plank connecting old dock pilings,
they stand, ragged, adolescent, legs apart,
lift stubby wings in an arc to dry.

Another flies in, lands too near his neighbor.
They spar for a moment, then sidestep away
in black huffs of disgust.

Spaced like a row of theater luminaires,
the cormorants perch and preen,
open their wings, flap, balance again.

Below them floats a red and white buoy.
Gulls cry, a boat speeds by, its fishing net
flying like a standard in the wind.

Madrone

Green and smooth
new naked skin

dries on twisted limbs
to rust, toughens
as it matures, then

cracks, curls, peels

like ragged scraps
from the buck's antlers,

littering brittle shreds
upon the earth,

leaving newness again.

Would the graven edges
of our spirits,

our worn indifference,

flake and fall away
through time's turnings

like the everlasting renewal
within the snake-branched

Madrone.

Comet

Three am, freezing darkness, we stumble
from our bunks, shiver into clothes,

out to crusted snow, look to the lake
past branches of the oak on the knoll,

into a sky thick with stars. And we see,
O God, a sweep of light streaming

through the heavens, blurred, iced
in a swirling, spark-strewn night.

Lips and cheeks numb with cold,
toes aching, we breath steam, stare

at this frosty halo, curve of tail, diffuse,
luminous, frozen like earth that morning,

forty-some years ago, an ice painting
still frozen in my accelerating sky.

Ice Bubbles

It's a long way down to earth
from the top of an ice cap –
two miles, more or less.
Core into time's cold press,
through glacial weight
of a hundred thousand snows,
days of woolly mammoths,
nights of cave paintings.
Capture the frozen bubbles
in slim cylinders, long tombs of time,
trapped samples of past atmospheres,
capsules of Neanderthal sky.

Bring this icy effervescence
to the surface,
this champagne of old air,
crystal blebs, rarest of draughts,
pre-agricultural, pre-industrial, pre-freon,
breezes long-forgotten,
catacombs of our ancient chemistry.

Sermermiut, Greenland

Turf remembers
peoples of the past.
Roots of arctic grasses
tangle from underhangs
like hair of the old ones.
Half-buried stones congregate
around spirit bones of Saqqat,
Dorset, Thule. Tools lie deep
in spongy middens, layers of peat
from four thousand snows.
Tourists stroll the boardwalk
among risings of their dwellings.
Bergs in the ice fjord
crack thunder.

Bob Hunger's Place
Isabella, Minnesota

Sing the old tunes
in firelight's circle of song,
harmony of guitar, flute.

Sing on the ski trail
across the pristine field
to the beaver pond,

untouched puffs of snow
on bushes and seedlings
as you race downhill,

out to the frozen lake.
Lie on your back in snow,
panting at thirty below.

Sing grace to the moon.
Her silver shines a path
to your home.

December Snowshoe

Trails wind
intimate with forest.
Ancient Ponderosa pines
of spiraling branches,
dark and spicy crevices,
guard winter birthing grounds
where the tree fetuses sleep.
From snowy fields they awaken,
emerge, uncurl. Elders
wear heavy snow shawls
on humble shoulders, bow
to their unseen creator.

winter

bleak frozen days
a longest night

chaos reigns
we're upside down

how do we escape
this age of iron

Janus' twin faces
look ahead, behind

no stopping
the wheel of Time

the mock king rules
but only for awhile

dark illuminates
keep keys at hand

your boots and staff
open new gates

your path is protected
the crossroads await

Karen Jones was born in Minneapolis, Minnesota and earned degrees from Carleton College and the University of Oregon. She taught special education for twenty-five years in Oregon public schools. Karen has published poetry in a variety of journals since 2015. *Seasons of Earth and Sky* is her first chapbook. She lives in Corvallis, Oregon.

www.ingramcontent.com/pod-product-compliance
Lightning Source LLC
LaVergne TN
LVHW041525070426
835507LV00013B/1833